DISCARD

THE HISTORY OF
ENERGY

Elaine Landau

TFCB

TWENTY-FIRST CENTURY BOOKS

Minneapolis

Dedication
For Darling Klara

Twenty-First Century Books
A division of Lerner Publishing Group
241 First Avenue North
Minneapolis, MN 55401 U.S.A.

Website address: www.lernerbooks.com

Library of Congress Cataloging-in-Publication Data

Landau, Elaine.
      The history of energy / by Elaine Landau.
          p.   cm. — (Major inventions through history)
      Includes bibliographical references and index.
      ISBN-13: 978—0—8225—3806—6 (lib. bdg. : alk. paper)
      ISBN-10: 0—8225—3806—7 (lib. bdg. : alk. paper)
      1. Power resources—Juvenile literature. I. Title. II. Series.
   TJ163.23.L358 2006
   641.042—dc22   2005003417

Manufactured in the United States of America
1 2 3 4 5 6 – DP – 11 10 09 08 07 06

CONTENTS

Introduction

It's an unbearably hot night. Suddenly the power in your house goes off. The air conditioner has stopped. Before long you feel really warm. Your computer won't work. The same is true for the TV. You would give anything for a cold soda. But the refrigerator isn't working and the sodas in it are already warm. All this happened because the electricity is off.

Electricity is a form of energy. Different forms and sources of energy exist all around us. Energy is the ability to do work. We use energy for everything we do. People use energy to run cars, trucks, and buses. We also use energy to barbecue burgers on an outdoor grill. It even takes energy for you to turn the pages of this book.

This book will discuss some sources and forms of energy. It will show how humans have invented different ways to harness this energy to make their lives easier. Energy has shaped our modern world.

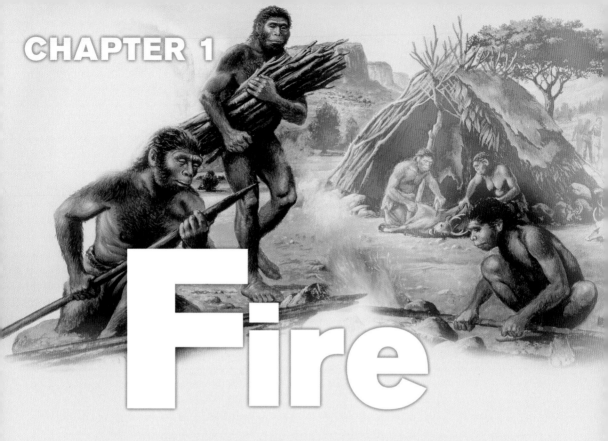

CHAPTER 1

Fire

Fire! It's a powerful word and an even more powerful force. If you heard it yelled out in a movie theater, you'd quickly head for an exit. Yet toasting marshmallows around a campfire can be the best part of a camping trip. In modern times, humans have learned to control fire. We know how to stop an unwanted fire as well as how to start one that will benefit us.

In the Beginning

Things were very different for early humans. Before humans learned

The age of *Homo erectus* begins.
ca. 1,600,000 B.C.

to create and control fire, life was certainly harder. Imagine having only uncooked plants and raw meat to eat. Not very tempting.

Fire was also a factor in deciding where to seek shelter. Often early humans stayed under cliffs or at the mouths of caves. Without fire, seeking shelter deep within a cave would not have been safe. Though it would have been warmer inside, it would also have been totally dark. Wild animals often lived in these dark places as well.

Of course, remaining in the open without a fire was risky too. This was especially true at night. Humans lack the claws and teeth to defeat a saber-toothed tiger or a cave lion. They couldn't outrun these animals, and early humans had few weapons. Many wild animals have a natural fear of fire, so a strong blaze could keep such unwelcome visitors away. This might mean life or death in some cases.

MYTHICAL VIEWS

Early humans believed that fire was magical. As time passed, ancient civilizations came up with different ideas about what fire was. Many cultures developed myths that included a fire god who demanded respect—otherwise he would take fire away forever.

Who First Harnessed Fire?

Anthropologists (scientists who study early humans) believe that *Homo erectus* was the first species of early humans to master fire. *Homo erectus* lived from about 1,600,000 to 250,000 years ago.

Homo erectus begins to master fire.

ca. 1,420,000 B.C.

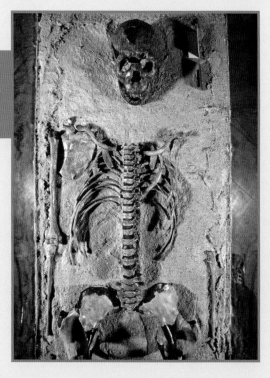

This fossilized *Homo erectus* skeleton was found in Kenya in 1984.

Anthropologists disagree on when and where humans first used fire. Yet most anthropologists agree that the effects of fire were discovered by chance. Some early people may have seen a forest fire caused by lightning and realized that it gave off warmth. Or perhaps someone accidentally dropped some animal meat in a brush fire begun by lightning. By the time someone took the meat from the fire, it would have been cooked.

So it's likely that early men and women used fire wherever they found it. When they came across a naturally occurring blaze, they'd take some smoldering sticks back to their camps. They would try to keep these fires going as long as possible by adding sticks or brush

The age of *Homo erectus* comes to an end.
ca. 250,000 B.C.

to fuel them. However, any rainstorm could put out these fires, and humans had no way to restart them—yet.

As time passed, early people learned to make their own fires. They discovered that the best way to do this is by creating sparks and intense heat. For example, rubbing pieces of flint (a kind of rock) together can create enough sparks to start a fire. Rubbing two pieces of dry wood together can produce enough heat to start a fire. For early humans, fire meant protection from cold. It also brought protection against wild animals on the prowl after dark. Early humans used fire to sharpen their wooden hunting spears. By heating the tip of the spear in a fire, they hardened its point. Using fire to cook food made many things taste better. Many plants are easier to digest when cooked. Cooking meat helped kill illness-causing bacteria too.

A View into the Past

Anthropologists learn about the past by studying fossils and other clues. Fossils are traces or remains of early people, animals, and plants that have been preserved in rock, sand, and other substances. In 1975 anthropologists were thrilled to find an almost complete human skeleton of a teenage *Homo erectus* boy in Africa. *Homo erectus* is the scientific name for the first human beings who walked erect, or on their hind legs. These scientists have found the remains of early campfires too. Such discoveries have helped us to know more about the importance of fire in the lives of early people.

Human beings begin to acquire fire-making skills.
ca. 7000 B.C.

Keeping the Home Fires Burning

Small groups of early humans banded together to survive. The center of their home life was the campfire. In the comfort and warmth of a toasty fire, early humans were able to relax. In time, they would share their experiences about the day's hunt. The taming of fire marked the start of community life.

LIGHT MY FIRE

The invention of matches made starting fires very easy. British pharmacist John Walker invented the first match in 1827. They were 3 feet (1 meter) long. Book matches were not created until 1889. American John Pusey invented them.

After discovering fire, early peoples began to slowly migrate to other regions and continents with cooler climates. This was possible because people had fire to help keep them warm. As a result, new parts of the world became populated.

In the centuries ahead, fire continued to be an important form of energy. People would depend on it to light their way in the darkness. Fire would be used to make pottery from clay. Fire remains essential to our lives. But in modern times, we create fire by burning coal, oil, and gasoline for industry, transportation, and home use.

Human beings use fire to clear brush and trees for farmland.

ca. 7000 B.C.

CHAPTER 2

Wind and Water

If you've ever stood in a fast-moving river or stream, you've felt the force of running water. If you've been out on a windy day, you've felt the power of the wind as well.

Suppose you lived in ancient Egypt in about 2000 B.C. Back then, watering crops took a lot of time and effort. Ancient peoples didn't have machines to direct the flow of water. One of the first inventions that did so was the waterwheel.

Waterpower

The waterwheel is a wheel mounted on an axle. The wheel has a set of paddles mounted on it. When placed in a stream or river, the rushing water hits the paddles, causing the wheel to turn. As the wheel turns, it creates mechanical energy. As early as 600 B.C., Egyptian farmers used waterwheels to irrigate, or bring water to, their crops during the dry season. They attached buckets to the wheel to scoop up and lift water.

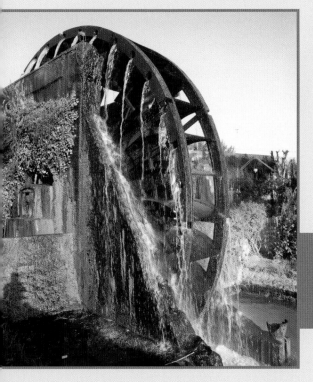

Irrigation is extremely important. It makes crop growth more certain, and people have fewer concerns about drought. Irrigation also allowed ancient farmers to expand their fields beyond riverbanks in some areas. More farms meant more food. And more food meant more people.

Waterwheels can be found throughout the world. This one is in Murcia, Spain.

Egyptian farmers use waterwheels to irrigate crops.
ca. 600 B.C.

Putting Wind to Work

By about A.D. 700, people in Persia (modern-day Iran) were putting the wind to work. The Persians designed some of the world's first windmills to power simple machines for irrigation and grinding grain.

These windmills were built inside of a building. The axle stretched from the floor to the ceiling. Fabric sails, or vanes, were attached to the axle. As wind blew inside the windows of the building, it pushed the vanes, causing them to turn the axle. The energy created could be used to irrigate crops or to turn grindstone wheels.

Dutch Windmills

Windmills were especially important in the Netherlands. The Netherlands are flat and have no rivers strong enough to create waterpower. Windmills were also vital because of the country's frequent floods. The energy generated by the windmills powered large scooping devices that scooped up the water.

Through the Years

Over the centuries, people improved the design of both windmills and waterwheels. By the 1600s, people were using both kinds of machines in many parts of Europe. Windmills from this period were attached to large towers. A large, propeller-shaped device held several sails, which captured the wind. As the wind blew, the sails turned, creating energy for irrigation or grinding.

Persians use early windmills.
ca. A.D. 700

Modern windmills have a similar look but are much more efficient. Instead of having sails, newer windmills have long, thin blades. Their towers are very tall and slender. These windmills are known as wind turbines. People use the energy they create to make electricity.

Yet wind turbines don't create a great deal of electricity. A single wind turbine will only produce enough electricity to supply one house or perhaps a small business. So to make the most of this energy source, people created wind farms with hundreds and even thousands of wind turbines.

California is home to the three largest wind farms in the world. One is along the Altamont Pass. Another is in the Tehachapi Mountains, and the third is along the San Gorgonio Pass in the south *(above)*. Each farm contains thousands of wind turbines.

People throughout much of
Europe use windmills.
ca. 1600s

Putting Water to Work

Hydropower, or waterpower, was an important energy source for North American colonists. (*Hydro* comes from the Greek word for water.) By the late 1770s, business owners were building cotton mills and textile (fabric) factories along the banks of rivers. Rushing water from these rivers turned large waterwheels that were connected to saw blades, looms, and other tools inside the factories. With waterpower, a good deal of work could be done at a fairly fast pace.

By the late 1800s, people were using hydropower to generate electricity. Water flows through a penstock (a tube or pipe) until it hits the blades of a wheel called a turbine. As the water spins the turbine, a machine called a generator transforms the energy into electricity. The result is hydroelectric power.

Swiftly flowing rivers or high waterfalls are good places to build hydroelectric plants. Another way to generate hydroelectric power is by building dams. Dams hold back flowing rivers. As they do this, they form lakes and reservoirs behind the dams. People working in the dam release some of the water from the reservoir. The rushing water spins the dam's turbines, generating electricity.

MONSTER WINDMILLS

Some modern wind turbines are huge. These wind machines are often as tall as a twenty-story building. The biggest machines have blades as long as a football field.

Hydropower is harnessed to power the Industrial Revolution in England.
late 1700s

The Grand Coulee Dam *(above)* near Spokane, Washington, is the United States' largest hydroelectric facility. It was built in the 1930s.

The United States' first hydroelectric power plant opened on September 30, 1882, on the Fox River near Appleton, Wisconsin. In the early 2000s, hydroelectric power plants supply energy for homes and businesses in many parts of the country.

The Good with the Bad

Both wind and waterpower have many benefits. They are inexpensive, do not produce waste materials, and do not pollute the air. Yet they

The first U.S. hydroelectric power plant opens on the Fox River in Appleton, Wisconsin.

1882

cannot be used everywhere. Some areas are not windy enough to support wind turbines. For example, only thirty-seven of the fifty U.S. states receive strong enough winds to make building wind farms worthwhile. Wind turbines are also noisy, and some people feel they are an ugly addition to a landscape. In addition, birds are sometimes caught and killed in the blades of wind turbines.

Hydroelectric power plants can be harmful to wildlife as well. When rivers are stopped or dammed, natural habitats are affected. Sometimes dams block fish from swimming upstream to their spawning grounds, where they reproduce. Nevertheless, unlike oil, these are renewable sources of energy. Many people hope these sources of power will be more widely used to keep things running.

RENEWABLE VS. NONRENEWABLE

Some sources of energy are renewable—they come from a source that won't run out. We all know that the sun will keep shining, rivers will keep flowing, and the wind will continue to blow. These are all important forms of energy that we count on.

Nonrenewable energy can be used up and would take a very long time to re-create. For example, coal and oil take millions of years to create. Yet most of the world relies on these nonrenewable sources because they are relatively cheap and reliable to extract and use.

Windpower is the fastest-growing source of energy in the United States.

early 2000s

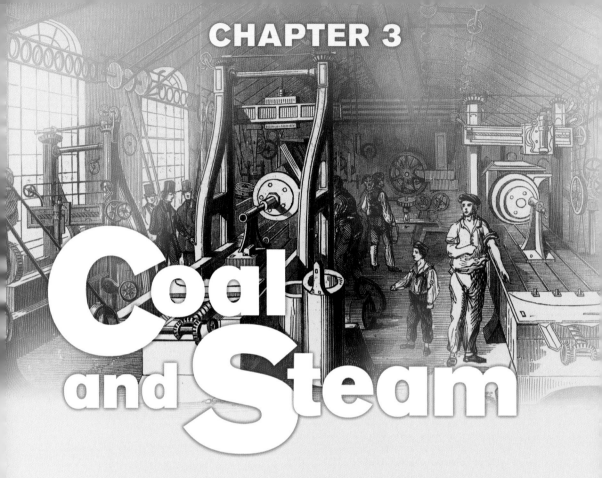

CHAPTER 3

Coal and Steam

The Romans, an empire based in Italy from about the first century B.C. to about the fifth century A.D., were great conquerors. While enlarging an already impressive empire, they traveled to different parts of the world. The troops and officials sent to these regions often had to deal with climates that were different from the warm weather in Italy. When they were in England, from about A.D. 100 to 200, the Romans figured out how to deal with the chilly weather there.

Romans in England build coal-burning furnaces to keep warm.

ca. A.D. 100

The Romans had already mastered some heating basics, including a type of furnace that they copied when they were in distant parts of the empire. In England the Romans did not use wood to fuel these furnaces. They found a fuel that burned hot, clean, and for longer periods—coal.

Coal is a fossil fuel. It is found beneath the earth's surface. Coal is a mineral formed over millions of years from the remains of plants and animals.

Early Uses

Throughout the ages, many different cultures used the energy that coal can create. In the 1300s, the Hopi Indians, who lived in what later became the southwestern United States, used coal to heat their homes and cook their food. They also made beautiful pottery from clay baked over the hot coals of a fire.

By the late 1600s, coal had become an extremely popular source of heating fuel in coal-rich England. In 1698 Englishman Thomas Savery designed an early steam engine. He used coal to fuel it. Savery's invention burned coal to bring large amounts of water to a boil. The blasts of steam given

A DIFFERENT KIND OF FIRE ENGINE

Thomas Savery's steam-driven machine was known as a fire engine. The coal-driven engine was actually invented as a tool for pumping water—out of coal mines!

Englishman Thomas Savery designs the first steam engine.

1698

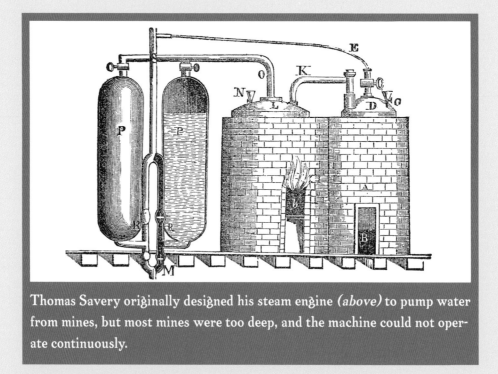

Thomas Savery originally designed his steam engine *(above)* to pump water from mines, but most mines were too deep, and the machine could not operate continuously.

off by the boiling water drove the engine. Savery's engine was a good start, but soon other inventors came up with more efficient coal-burning engines.

Steaming Ahead

In 1765 James Watt, a Scotsman, was asked to repair a steam engine. After studying the machine, he did more than repair it—he rebuilt and enhanced it, making it more powerful, efficient, and

Scotsman James Watt
develops a more powerful
and efficient steam engine.

1765

reliable. Watt's engine soon became the model after which all steam engines were built.

Watt's new steam engines became essential to Britain's developing industries. To power textile looms, steam engines worked better than waterwheels. Machinery powered by steam was faster and cheaper. So yarn could be spun and cloth could be woven faster and more cheaply.

Watt's engine helped to power Britain's Industrial Revolution in the early 1800s. Britain's textile, shipbuilding, iron, and steel industries boomed. British factories manufactured goods that were once made by hand. As a result, more and more people left Britain's countryside to find work in city factories. In turn, Britain's cities grew very fast. The changes transformed the country into an urban, industrial nation. Later, the Industrial Revolution spread to many other European countries, as well as to the United States.

IRON AND STEEL

Many heavy machines were made of iron. To create iron, ironworkers use extremely hot chambers called blast furnaces to separate iron from iron ore (the rock iron is found in). In its natural form, coal cannot be used to fuel these blast furnaces because coal contains sulfur, a chemical that makes iron too brittle. However, in 1709 Englishman Abraham Darby invented a process to extract, or remove, the sulfur from coal. Coal without sulfur is known as coke. Darby's important invention allowed people to produce huge amounts of iron. Later on, coke was also used to make steel—a tough metal that combines iron and carbon.

Coal-burning steam engines help drive the Industrial Revolutions in Great Britain and other countries.
ca. 1800

Steam for Transportation

Meanwhile, as this revolution in industry was taking place, a revolution was also occurring in transportation. In 1787 U.S. inventor John Fitch made the first successful steamboat journey on the Delaware River in the eastern United States. Twenty years later, in 1807, another American, Robert Fulton, sailed a newer and better steamboat on a 150-mile (241-kilometer) journey from New York City to Albany, New York. Less than ten years after Fulton's historic journey, steamboats were offering passenger service on several waterways around the country. The invention of the steamboat was a major milestone in human progress. It allowed people and goods to travel without relying on wind, water currents, or rowing.

Other exciting developments were also taking place. More

ROBERT FULTON

Though Robert Fulton (1765–1815) was an inventor, he didn't invent the steamboat. Yet he did a great deal to advance this form of transportation. In 1807 Fulton oversaw the construction of a steamboat known as the *Clermont*. Fulton did not design its steam engine himself—instead, he got a steam engine from James Watt and adjusted it for the *Clermont*.

Fulton used the *Clermont* to provide regular passenger service on New York's Hudson River. It was the first steamboat to do so. Few thought that Fulton's idea would work. As people saw steam coming from the vessel, many thought it would blow up. But they were wrong—the *Clermont* proved to be a success. In time, steamboat travel would be an important form of transportation.

John Fitch makes the first steamboat journey in the United States.

1787

improvements to steam engines produced machines light enough and powerful enough to pull vehicles on land. When placed on tracks, these locomotives traveled across the land much faster and more easily than ever before. Like the steamboat, the locomotive caused a revolution. Before steam-powered trains, most heavy cargo had to be moved by boat. So most cities and towns were along rivers or other bodies of water. Railway networks allowed more people to move inland, away from water.

Steam-powered trains changed the way people lived. Cargo, and people, could move faster and farther than ever before.

Colonel John Stevens is granted the first railroad charter in the United States.

1815

The transcontinental railroad, linking the east and west coasts of the United States, is completed.

1869

Over the years, the role of coal as a fuel for steam-powered engines became increasingly vital. By the late 1880s, steamboats and steam-powered trains had become the nation's major forms of transportation. Gone were the days of pioneer wagon trains taking months to cross the country. Steam-powered locomotives traveled from coast-to-coast in a week.

A NONRENEWABLE FUEL

Coal is called a nonrenewable fuel because only a limited amount of it exists. Creating coal takes millions of years. It's estimated that if we continue using coal at our current rate, the world's coal supply will last for about the next two hundred years.

In that decade, U.S. power companies began to use coal to generate electricity. Power plants burned coal to boil water. This produced steam to turn the turbines of electricity-producing generators.

Coal remains a very important fuel in the twenty-first century. More than 90 percent of the coal produced in the United States is used for electricity. Each year the United States mines about 1 million tons (907,185 metric tons) of coal.

The U.S. coal industry employs about eighty thousand coal miners.

early 2000s

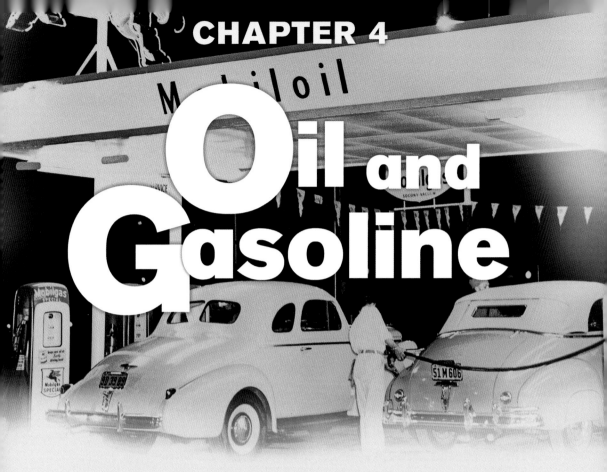

CHAPTER 4

Oil and Gasoline

Cars, motorcycles, and many trucks all have one thing in common—they run on gasoline. Take a moment to think about it. Can you picture our world without gas? We depend on gasoline-fueled vehicles to go places as well as to have things brought to us.

From beneath the Ground

Gasoline is one of many products that come from petroleum, or oil. Oil, like coal, is a fossil fuel. It is nonrenewable—only a limited

Mesopotamians use petroleum to caulk ships.
ca. 4000 B.C.

amount of it exists. Oil is formed over millions of years from the decayed remains of countless tiny marine animals and plants. When extracted from the earth, crude (unprocessed) oil is a foul-smelling, yellowish to black substance.

People have used oil for many different purposes. The ancient Egyptians used oil for medicine. Around 4000 B.C., people in Mesopotamia (modern-day Iraq) used oil to caulk, or waterproof, their ships. By 2000 B.C., the Chinese were burning oil products for home heating and lighting. Some North American Indian tribes also used oil. In the northeast, the Seneca and Iroquois used it for body paint and special ceremonial fires.

Accidental Use

Spanish explorers coming to America in 1543 sometimes accidentally stepped in oil seeps on the ground. They soon discovered that this strange sticky substance could be useful. It waterproofed their boots.

Oozing out of the Earth

In the 1750s, settlers in northwestern Pennsylvania and western New York often found oil on their property. Such discoveries usually came when people were digging wells for water. When thick, sticky crude oil came oozing out of the earth instead, the settlers were left with a mess to clean up.

By the mid-1800s, Americans were beginning to develop many uses for oil. For example, kerosene—a fuel made from oil—had

People in China burn oil products for home heating and lighting.

ca. 2000 B.C.

In the late 1800s, many streetlamps in large cities were lit with kerosene.

become a popular fuel for lighting homes, streets, and businesses. Oil also makes an excellent lubricant for machines.

In the late 1850s, a number of ambitious Americans were setting up drilling operations with the hope of finding oil. Colonel Edwin Drake was one of the first of these oil explorers. In the summer of 1859, Drake began drilling for oil in Titusville, Pennsylvania. At first, the work went slowly and there were lots of problems. Before long, Drake's money ran out and he was forced to borrow more to continue the project. The project soon earned a nickname—Drake's Folly.

By late summer, the situation did not look any better. On August 27, 1859, Drake received a letter from one of the company's major investors. The letter instructed Drake to close down the site and send his workers home. But Drake struck oil that

Colonel Edwin Drake begins drilling for oil in western Pennsylvania.
1859

Colonel Edwin Drake had never really served as a colonel in any military organization. He just used the title to impress others.

very same day! People who had called the drilling operation Drake's Folly were wrong. The oil, which became known as black gold, sold for twenty dollars a barrel.

Word of Drake's success spread like lightning. Thousands rushed to north-western Pennsylvania to seek their fortunes drilling for oil. The quiet farming region was soon alive with the sound of hundreds of active oil wells. In the decade to come, a new invention would come along that would cause the demand for oil to skyrocket.

Horseless Carriages

On September 20, 1893, on the outskirts of Springfield, Massachusetts, bicycle mechanic Frank Duryea test-drove the horseless carriage that he and his brother Charles had built. Duryea only drove the car a short distance, but his journey was a giant leap for mankind. The Duryea horseless carriage was one of the first— if not *the* first—gasoline-powered automobiles ever built and driven in the United States. Within months, the brothers had founded the Duryea Motorcar Company.

German engineer Gottlieb Daimler develops one of the first gasoline-powered combustion engines.

1885

The Duryea brothers and many others saw that the automobile was the way of the future. And the rise of gasoline-powered cars meant a rise in the demand for oil. By the turn of the century, more than eight thousand automobiles were registered in the United States.

As the number of cars on U.S. roads continued to grow, demand for oil increased dramatically. The success in Pennsylvania was followed by the 1901 oil boom in Texas. Ambitious oil barons also found and tapped oil in California, Oklahoma, and Louisiana. These developments marked the beginning of the modern oil industry.

From the Ground to the Customer

Crude oil has few uses in its natural state. Refineries use a complicated process to separate oil into many different products, including gasoline, lubrication oil, diesel fuel, home heating fuel, and asphalt.

Once oil is refined, the gasoline it yields must be transported and sold to consumers. Yet in the early 1900s, gas stations did not exist. At first, motorists purchased their gas from bulk depots. To protect the general public from gasoline explosions or fires, these establishments were located outside of crowded areas.

RUNNING ON EMPTY

Most early automobiles did not have gas gauges. Motorists had to guess how much gas was in the tank by looking inside or tapping the tank and listening to how hollow it sounded.

U.S. automaker Henry Ford introduces the Model T Ford, the first car that was affordable to the general public.

1908

BAD GAS

Before the invention of the automobile, most crude oil was used to make kerosene. After refining, a single barrel of crude oil yields about 3 percent kerosene. Much of the rest—40 percent—is gasoline. Before the automobile era, gasoline was considered a waste product—too dangerous to store and too flammable to use for heating or lighting homes.

Bulk depots sold gas in tin cans. Motorists poured the gas into their cars using a funnel. It was messy and dangerous. In 1905 Harry Grenner and Clem Laessig formed the Automobile Gasoline Company in Saint Louis, Missouri. The two men stored gas in large aboveground tanks. Hoses attached to the tanks fed gasoline straight into waiting automobiles. The first gas station was born! Meanwhile, a number of U.S. inventors were developing gas pumps to measure the amount of gas going into the car.

As demand grew, gas stations soon spread throughout the country. Gas stations became a part of the U.S. landscape and a part of U.S. culture.

Oil Makes the World Go 'Round

By the 1950s, the oil industry had reached around the world. Oil wells were pumping millions of barrels of oil from every continent in the world except Antarctica. Offshore wells extracted the black gold from deep beneath the ocean floor. Huge ships called tankers carry oil by sea. These giant vessels can carry millions of gallons of oil around the

Major oil production begins in Saudi Arabia. The kingdom would go on to become the world's leading oil producer.

1946

world. Pipelines carry oil on land. The United States' pipeline system is the largest in the world. It has more than 2 million miles (3,218,688 km) of pipelines.

Blessing or Curse?

The world is dependent on oil. With jet fuel, we can hop on a plane and be in another part of the world within hours. Many homes, businesses, and schools are warm in the winter because they are heated with oil. Having oil allows us to live more comfortably.

Yet there's a downside to our ongoing need for this energy source. Through the years, brutal wars have been fought over oil-rich lands. Burning oil creates air pollution as well.

Oil is a nonrenewable resource. And not all scientists agree on how much oil is left in the world. In fact, some studies show that oil production may decline before the end of this century due to the lack of supply. Other studies note that some areas of the world have yet to be explored for oil.

TITANIC TANKER

The oil tanker *Jahre Viking* is the largest ship in the world. She is 1,503 feet (458 m) long and 226 feet (69 m) across at her widest point. Built in Japan in the late 1970s, the *Jahre Viking* weighs more than 500,000 tons (more than 453,000 metric tons) when fully loaded and can carry more than 4 million barrels of oil. Despite her massive size, the ship has a crew of only forty people. Crew members use bicycles to get from one part of the ship to another.

World oil production hovers at 22 billion barrels a year.

2005

CHAPTER 5
Electricity

Most Americans take electricity for granted. We use it to surf the Internet, light lamps, and run the dishwasher. But human beings have only been enjoying such luxury for a little more than a century.

In Days Gone By

People have long been fascinated by electricity. Ancient people saw lightning in the sky and thought it was the work of some powerful god. Around 600 B.C., the ancient Greeks did some early experiments with electricity. They rubbed a piece of amber (a fossilized

People in Greece perform experiments with electricity.
ca. 600 B.C.

tree product) against a fur cloth and saw that it attracted small pieces of straw. These were some of the first-known experiments with static electricity—the same force you experience when you touch a wall after rubbing your feet on carpet.

In A.D. 1600, Dr. William Gilbert, the physician to Queen Elizabeth I of England, performed some experiments of his own. He found that some items, such as glass and wax, acted like amber under similar conditions. Gilbert called this independent natural force electricity. He took the word from the Greek term *elektron*.

The great U.S. inventor, printer, writer, and statesman Ben Franklin believed that lightning was a naturally occurring flow of electricity. To prove his idea, he tied an iron key to the string of a kite and flew it on a stormy night in 1752. Legend has it that lightning struck the kite. When the electrical charge traveled down to the key, Franklin is said to have received a shock. Franklin's experiments—and the writings that he published describing them—caused a sensation in America and

WHAT'S ELECTRICITY, ANYWAY?

When discussing electricity, it helps to know about atoms. Everything around us is made of tiny particles known as atoms. Each atom has a center called a nucleus. Within the nucleus are particles called protons and neurons. Other particles called electrons travel around the nucleus at a very fast rate. An outside force has the ability to bump or push electrons to different atoms. This electron action produces electricity.

Benjamin Franklin performs his famous kite-in-a-thunderstorm experiment.

1752

This painting depicts Franklin's famous lightning experiment. A similar experiment had already been conducted in France with an iron rod atop a tall building, but Franklin hadn't yet heard of it.

Europe. Franklin's ideas got more people thinking about electricity. They wondered if this powerful force could ever be harnessed.

Putting Electricity to Work

By the mid-1800s, scientists had discovered the relationship between electricity and magnetism. These discoveries led to the inventions of the first dynamos, or generators, which used magnetism to create electricity.

Thomas Edison, inventor of
the lightbulb, is born.
1847

Nikola Tesla, developer of
alternating current, is born.
1856

In 1879 U.S. inventor Thomas Edison made another historic breakthrough when he unveiled his design for the lightbulb. Yet lightbulbs weren't much use without electricity to power them. So Edison went about building the very first commercial power station. His work led to the opening of the Pearl Street Power Station in New York City on September 4, 1882. The station delivered electricity via underground cables to homes and offices within a 1-square-mile (2.6 sq. km) area. Within a year, the station was serving more than four hundred customers and lighting more than ten thousand lamps.

WHAT'S A WATT?

Have you ever changed a lightbulb and noticed that it was marked 40, 60, 75, or 100 watts? Units of electricity are measured in watts. These units were named to honor the steam engine inventor James Watt, even though he never conducted experiments with electricity.

Word quickly spread about Edison's safe, reliable, and efficient form of lighting. People in other parts of the United States and in Europe asked Edison to create electrical systems for their cities. By the late 1880s, Edison had built several other small power stations in cities across the country.

Important Advances in Electric Power

The growing electric industry took another step forward with the work of U.S. inventor Nikola Tesla. Tesla used an alternating current

Edison opens the Pearl Street Power Station in New York City.

1882

This model of Edison's Pearl Street Power Station is on view at the Edison National Historic Site in West Orange, New Jersey.

(AC) to send electricity longer distances. (Edison's power stations used a different method, known as direct current.) Alternating current is an electric flow that reverses its direction at regular intervals (spaces). Tesla felt that AC was a better choice for supplying electricity to people. AC could be transformed to higher or lower voltages. A higher voltage sent out from a distant power station could be lowered to a safer voltage for home use.

George Westinghouse begins to install hydroelectric generators at Niagara Falls, New York.

1893

Another U.S. inventor, George Westinghouse, purchased the rights to Tesla's work. In 1893 Westinghouse won the contract to install three very large generators at Niagara Falls in upstate New York. He built on Tesla's work by developing a transformer. Transformers allowed electricity to be efficiently transmitted over long distances. Soon Tesla's AC current became the standard for transmitting electrical power.

By the 1930s, nearly every U.S. city had electrical service. In the 1930s, President Franklin D. Roosevelt launched an ambitious plan to bring electricity to the nation's farms and small towns.

The Growth of the Grids

Modern power-generating stations are linked through a system known as power grids, which carry electricity at extremely high voltages. The power from

ELECTRICITY FOR EVERYONE

By the 1930s, virtually all urban areas in the United States had electricity. But many rural areas did not. The highest profits for energy came from providing electricity to cities or heavily populated areas. Power companies didn't see much profit in putting up electric lines to serve a small number of people. Electric company investors also feared that in some regions many farmers might not be able to afford electricity.

President Roosevelt believed that all Americans should have electricity. In 1935 he helped to create the Rural Electric Administration. This government agency brought electricity to rural areas at reasonable prices. It bettered the lives of millions of farmers.

President Roosevelt launches the Rural Electric Administration.
1935

the generating stations flows through the transmission lines to smaller regional and neighborhood substations. There the high-voltage electricity is switched to a current that is safe for home and office use.

The U.S. power grid consists of more than 150,000 miles (241,402 km) of high-voltage transmission lines. The grid links towns and cities across the United States and much of Canada.

The United States generates approximately 3,858 billion kilowatt hours of electricity each year.

2005

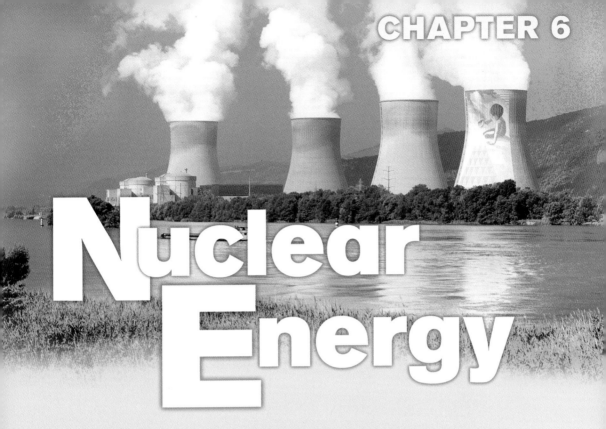

CHAPTER 6

Nuclear Energy

On August 6, 1945, a lone U.S. bomber, nicknamed the *Enola Gay*, dropped a giant bomb over Hiroshima, Japan. When the bomb exploded several thousand feet over the city, it created a massive fireball that instantly killed tens of thousands of Japanese. Many more died later from a kind of sickness called radiation poisoning. The first atomic bomb attack had just

DROPPING THE BOMB

"My God, what have we done?"
—Robert Lewis, copilot of the *Enola Gay*, which dropped a nuclear bomb over Hiroshima, Japan, in 1945.

The United States enters World War II and begins work to build an atomic bomb.

1941

The 9,700-pound (4,400-kilogram) atomic bomb that was dropped over Hiroshima was nicknamed Little Boy. The 10,800-pound (4,899 kg) bomb that was dropped over Nagasaki, Japan, two days later was nicknamed Fat Man. Pictured at left is the mushroom cloud from Fat Man.

taken place. While the event soon brought an end to World War II (1939—1945), it also marked the beginning of the nuclear age.

Atomic bombs use the power of the atom to cause tremendous destruction. But the power of the atom can also be used to make electricity. Nuclear power is released as the result of changes in the nuclei (core or center) of an element (substance) such as uranium. Using uranium as a fuel, nuclear engineers rely on a very complicated process called fission to unleash nuclear energy. During the process, the uranium's nuclei split into tiny pieces, or fragments, releasing tremendous energy.

After World War II, scientists explored the peacetime uses of nuclear energy. In 1954 the U.S. Navy launched the USS *Nautilus*,

U.S. atomic bombs kill approximately 170,000 Japanese in two separate attacks.

1945

the world's first nuclear-powered submarine. Powered by a nuclear reactor, nuclear submarines can stay submerged beneath the water for months at a time and can travel for years without refueling. Nuclear energy has also been used to power ships as well as aircraft carriers and spacecraft.

While the *Nautilus* was sailing on its first missions, nuclear power plants were being built in the United States and Great Britain. The world's first commercial nuclear plant opened in 1956 in northern Great Britain. The following year, the United States opened its own nuclear power plant in Shippingport, Pennsylvania.

The USS *Nautilus* surfaces outside New York City.

The Soviet Union develops
its own atomic bomb.
1949

Since then more than 435 nuclear reactors have been built in more than thirty countries. The United States produces more nuclear energy than any other nation. Nuclear power generates about 20 percent of the United States' electricity.

Nuclear power plants use nuclear reactions to produce heated water. The heated water creates steam. The steam turns a set of steam turbines. These turbines produce electricity.

Nuclear Medicine

Nuclear energy benefits society through nuclear medicine. Doctors use certain forms of low-level radiation to kill cancer cells or stop their spread. Sometimes doctors use radiation therapy to shrink cancerous tumors before surgery. Other times, doctors use radiation to kill any remaining cancer cells after surgery.

Many of the best medical scanning and imaging machines use radioactive substances. In 1973 physicist Robert S. Ledley invented the full-body computer tomography (CT) scanner. CT scans allow doctors to view a body's soft tissue in great detail. They are extremely helpful in detecting cancer, heart disease, bone disease, and other illnesses.

Magnetic resonance imaging (MRI) creates detailed images of internal body structures, such as the brain. It can also zero in on tiny pieces of tissue. Positron emission tomography (PET) scans can detect abnormal cell activity. This can often be a sign of cancer. They can sometimes spot a problem at an early stage, allowing doctors to act sooner.

The first nuclear power plant goes online (into service) in Great Britain.
1956

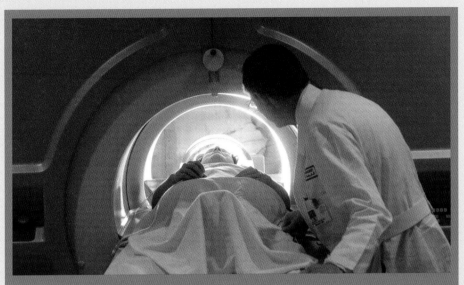

Many advances in modern medicine have been made thanks to nuclear energy. One such advance is the CT scanner, shown above.

Danger Ahead!

Nuclear reactions don't just create heat for electricity. They also create radiation and radioactive waste. Radiation is the particles and rays given off during a nuclear reaction. They can be extremely harmful, even deadly. High doses of it can cause radiation sickness. Exposure to radiation can also cause such diseases as cancer. People exposed to high levels of radiation may also have children with birth defects.

All nuclear power plants are designed with safety in mind. Yet accidents have happened. The most famous nuclear accident in

North America—a partial meltdown—took place at the Three Mile Island nuclear power plant in Middletown, Pennsylvania, on March 28, 1979. Nuclear meltdowns occur when a nuclear reactor's core is severely overheated.

Seven years later, in 1986, a far more serious accident took place at the Chernobyl nuclear power plant in the eastern European country of Ukraine. An experiment caused an explosion that damaged the nuclear reactor. A large amount of radiation was released into the atmosphere. Thirty-one people soon died due to burns and radiation sickness. Hundreds more were injured. The accident spread radioactive particles for hundreds of

Fifteen years after the Chernobyl disaster, scientists test the radiation level outside the concrete building that houses Chernobyl's ruined nuclear reactor.

An explosion at the Chernobyl power plant spreads radioactive material over northern Ukraine and Belarus.

1986

miles across Ukraine and its neighbor, Belarus.

The accidents at Three Mile Island and Chernobyl increased worldwide fear and distrust of nuclear power. In the United States, the U.S. Nuclear Regulatory Commission (NRC) government closely regulates all nuclear power plants.

The NRC also oversees the storage of nuclear waste in several locations throughout the United States. Nuclear waste is the material leftover from spent (used up) nuclear fuel. Spent nuclear fuel is extremely radioactive and toxic. It remains radioactive for hundreds of years and must be stored in special containers to prevent leaking. In the mid-2000s, nuclear power remains a key, though controversial source of energy. Its long-term future remains uncertain.

NUCLEAR WASTE

A nuclear reactor creates from 20 to 30 tons (18 to 27 metric tons) of high-level nuclear waste every year. This waste is stored in pools that look like huge swimming pools. The water cools the waste and acts as a shield to prevent the spread of radiation. As time passes, nuclear waste becomes less radioactive and is then stored in a dry storage area. The nuclear waste is sealed in special containers reinforced with concrete. In the mid-2000s, spent nuclear fuel is stored at the plant where it is made. However, the U.S. government is working to build a nuclear waste storage site at Yucca Mountain, Nevada, where much of the nation's nuclear waste can be shipped for storage.

Epilogue

Energy makes the world go around. Harnessing energy allows us to have fuller and more comfortable lives. But things may get even better in the future. Some exciting new developments are taking shape in the field of energy.

Solar energy taps the limitless power of the sun. Human beings have been using solar energy to produce electricity for decades. Special devices, called solar panels, absorb the rays of the sun and convert them into energy for electricity. One of the best things about solar energy is that it's free. It's also renewable—we all know that the sun keeps shining. Yet we cannot use the sun for energy when it is cloudy or at night. Because of this, some people use solar energy as a backup energy source. When available, they use solar energy instead of energy from another source.

Geothermal energy is another growing energy option. Geothermal energy is heat from beneath the earth's surface. The earth's interior is extremely hot. Geothermal power stations use the earth's natural heat to create steam. In turn, the steam turns turbines that produce electricity.

Biomass is another energy source that is growing in popularity. Biomass is energy from plant materials, such as wood. These materials are renewable and burn much cleaner than coal or oil.

Some countries, such as Canada, are planning to create "energy plantations." Farmers on these plantations would plant fast-growing trees for use as fuel. After the trees are chopped down and cut into small chips for fuel, new trees would be planted to replace them. Burning waste and garbage is another potential biomass fuel.

Fuel cells might be the most exciting future source of energy. Hydrogen fuel cells convert hydrogen and oxygen into water. This conversion creates electricity. A single fuel cell only produces a small amount of electricity. Therefore, a large number of fuel cells are put together in a stack. Many people believe that fuel cells will one day replace gasoline-burning engines in cars.

Our major energy sources may change in the years ahead. Scientists are actively exploring many different sources of energy. Someday your garbage may never get to a landfill. Instead, it may be burned for your warmth and comfort.

TIMELINE

ca. 4000 B.C. Mesopotamians use oil to caulk their ships.

ca. 2000 B.C. The Chinese burn oil products for home heating and lighting.

ca. 600 B.C. Waterwheels are used in areas with little rain to water crops.

ca. 100 B.C Waterwheels are used to create energy to grind grain.

ca. A.D. 700 One of the earliest windmills used to grind grain is created in Persia (modern-day Iran).

1300s The Hopi Indians use coal to heat their homes and cook their food.

1543 Spanish explorers in America accidentally step in oil seeps on the ground. They find that this sticky substance waterproofs their boots.

1600s Windmills are used to capture wind power in Europe. Coal becomes popular as a fuel in England.

1698 Englishman Thomas Savery designs an early steam engine.

1700s Waterpower is used by growing industries in the United States as an energy source .

1709 A new process is invented to remove sulfur from coal. The substance left is known as coke and is used in manufacturing iron.

1752 Ben Franklin conducts his famous "kite in a thunderstorm" experiment to test electricity.

1765 James Watt improves the design of the steam engine. His design becomes the model for future steam engines.

1783 The first paddlewheel boats navigate Europe's waterways.

1815 Colonel John Stevens is granted the first railroad charter in North America.

1859 Colonel Edwin Drake strikes oil in Titusville, Pennsylvania.

1879 Thomas Edison invents the lightbulb.

1882 Thomas Edison develops the first successful electric generating station fueled by coal.

1893 George Westinghouse is awarded a contract to harness the water-power at Niagara Falls, New York.

1893 The Duryea brothers test-drive their very first horseless carriage near Springfield, Massachusetts.

1899 Thirty U.S. automobile manufacturers produce twenty-five thousand cars.

1901 The Texas oil boom begins.

1935 President Franklin D. Roosevelt creates the Rural Electric Administration.

1941 The United States enters World War II and begins building an atomic bomb.

1945 The United States drops two atomic bombs on Japan, leading to the end of World War II.

1954 The U.S. Navy launches the USS *Nautilus*, the first nuclear-powered submarine.

1956 The world's first large-scale nuclear power plant opens in northern Great Britain.

1973 Physicist Robert S. Ledley unveils the full-body computer tomography (CT) scanner.

1979 An accident occurs at the Three Mile Island nuclear power plant in Pennsylvania.

1986 An explosion occurs at the Chernobyl nuclear power plant in Ukraine.

1990s The United States and other nations introduce new cleaner-burning gasolines.

2000 More than 90 percent of the coal produced in the United States is used for electricity.

2005 Manufacturers are selling hydrogen fuel cells for use as batteries in electronics equipment such as cameras and laptop computers.

GLOSSARY

biomass: energy created by the burning of dead waste materials, such as wood, other plant matter, and garbage

flint: a hard, gray stone that makes sparks when struck

fossil fuel: sources of energy, such as coal and petroleum, that are derived from fossils

fossils: the preserved remains or traces of plants or animals from millions of years ago

fuel cells: devices that create energy through the process of converting hydrogen into water

geothermal energy: energy created by tapping the heat of the earth's interior

hydroelectric: electricity created by the force of rushing water

irrigate: supply water to crops by artificial means

nonrenewable energy: energy sources—such as coal and oil—of which the earth has only a limited supply

nuclear reactor: a large machine that produces nuclear power

penstock: a pipe used to direct the flow of water

petroleum: a thick, oily liquid found beneath the earth's surface that is used to make gasoline, kerosene, heating oil, asphalt, and many other products

radiation: particles that are sent out from a radioactive substance

radiation poisoning: an often deadly illness that is caused by exposure to radiation. Symptoms include vomiting, diarrhea, internal bleeding, hair loss, and death.

renewable energy: energy sources—such as windpower, hydroelectric power, and solar power—that will not run out

turbines: machines that are driven by water, steam, or gas passing through the blades of a wheel that make it revolve

Selected Bibliography

Berger, John. *Charging Ahead: The Business of Renewable Energy and What It Means for America*. New York: Henry Holt, 1997.

Berinstein, Paula. *Alternative Energy: Facts, Statistics, and Issues*. Westport, CT: Oryx Press, 2001.

Bodansky, David. *Nuclear Energy: Principles, Practices, and Prospects*. Melville, NY: American Institute of Physics, 1996.

Cassedy, Edward S. *Prospects for Sustainable Energy: A Critical Assessment*. West Nyack, NY: Cambridge University Press, 2000.

Ewing, Rex A. *Power with Nature: Solar and Wind Energy Demystified*. Masonville, CO: Pixyjack Press, 2003.

Goodstein, David. *Out of Gas: All You Need to Know about the End of the Age of Oil*. New York: Norton & Company, 2004.

Klare, Michael T. *Blood and Oil: The Dangers and Consequences of America's Growing Petroleum Dependency*. New York: Metropolitan Books, 2004.

McNamara, Will. *The California Energy Crisis: Lessons for a Deregulating Industry*. Tulsa: PennWell Corp, 2002.

Morris, Robert. *The Environmental Case for Nuclear Power: Economic, Medical, and Political Considerations*. St. Paul: Paragon House, 2000.

Patel, Mukund R. *Wind and Solar Power Systems*. Boca Raton, FL: CRC, 1999.

Pyne, Stephen J. *Fire: A Brief History*. Seattle: University of Washington Press, 2001.

Roberts, Paul. *The End of Oil: On the Edge of a Perilous New World*. Boston: Houghton Mifflin, 2004.

Scheer, Hermann. *The Solar Economy: Renewable Energy for a Sustainable Global Future*. London: Earthscan Publications, 2002.

Schobert, Harold H. *Energy and Society: An Introduction*. New York: Taylor & Francis Group, 2001.

FURTHER READING AND WEBSITES

Alliant Energy Kids
  http://www.alliantenergykids.com
  This colorful website provides fun information about energy.

Challoner, Jack. *Energy*. New York: DK Publishing, 2000.
  Illustrated with color photos and 3-D models, this Eyewitness book explores the various forms of energy we use.

Cooper, Christopher. *Matter*. New York: DK Publishing, 1999.
  Packed with photographs and diagrams, this Eyewitness book covers such areas as the use of electricity and the laws of force, energy, and matter.

Daley, Michael J. *Nuclear Power: Promise or Peril?* Minneapolis: Lerner Publications Company, 1997.
  Explore the many controversial issues that surround nuclear power.

Dommermuth-Costa, Carol. *Nikola Tesla: A Spark of Genius*. Minneapolis: Lerner Publications Company, 1994.
  Learn more about the brilliant Croatian-born inventor who developed the technology that harnessed AC current and much, much more.

Dr. E's Energy Lab
  http://www.eere.energy.gov/kids/
  This site provides a fun visit to a cartoonlike energy lab where young people learn about different forms of energy.

Fleisher, Paul. *Matter and Energy: Principles of Matter and Thermodynamics*. Minneapolis: Lerner Publications Company, 2002.
  Expand your knowledge of matter and energy in the book from Lerner's Secrets of the Universe series.

———. *Relativity and Quantum Mechanics: Principles of Modern Physics*. Minneapolis: Lerner Publications Company, 2002.
  This volume in Lerner's Secrets of the Universe series explores Einstein's important theory of relativity, which led the way toward understanding how to tap atomic energy.

Gibson, Diane. *Geothermal Power*. North Mankato, MN: Smart Apple Media, 2000.
  This book provides an interesting overview of geothermal power.

Graham, Ian. *Water Power*. Austin, TX: Raintree, 1999.
  This well-illustrated book on waterpower describes how this important energy source is harnessed and put to work.

Kids' Pages
  http://www.mms.gov/mmskids/
  The Kids' Pages at this Minerals Management Service website offer information on ocean energy—including drilling for oil in the ocean and exploring wave energy.

McPherson, Stephanie Sammartino. *Ordinary Genius: The Story of Albert Einstein*. Minneapolis: Carolrhoda Books, Inc., 1995.
  The fascinating life and career of the brilliant scientist Albert Einstein is chronicled in this book from Carolrhoda's Trailblazer biography series.

Tagliaferro, Linda. *Thomas Edison: Inventor of the Age of Electricity*. Minneapolis: Lerner Publications Company, 2003.
  This engaging biography follows the remarkable life of inventor Thomas Edison and includes information about his development of the lightbulb and the Pearl Street Power Station.

Woods, Michael, and Mary B. Woods. *Ancient Agriculture: From Foraging to Farming*. Minneapolis: Lerner Publications Company, 2000.
  Learn more about ancient agricultural techniques, including early forms of irrigation, from this volume in Lerner's Ancient Technology series.

——. *Ancient Machines: From Wedges to Waterwheels*. Minneapolis: Lerner Publications Company, 2000.
  Expand your knowledge about waterwheels and other ancient inventions with this volume in Lerner's Ancient Technology series.

COVER AND CHAPTER OPENER PHOTO CAPTIONS

Cover Top: This log cabin and waterwheel was the first electrical generator in Washington State. Bottom: Turbines in Hoover Dam

pp. 4–5 This view of Chicago, Illinois, at night shows an electrical power grid, seen in the parallel lines of light.

p. 6 An artist's rendering of early humans gathered around a fire

p. 11 A pair of nineteenth-century Dutch windmills.

p. 18 A railway engine factory in Great Britain during the late 1800s

p. 25 As automobile use spread across the United States in the early 1900s, gas stations such as this one popped up in their wake.

p. 32 Everything in this modern kitchen is run by electricity.

p. 39 A nuclear power station on the Rhone River in France

pp. 46–47 A solar energy research plant in Almeria, Spain

ABOUT THE AUTHOR

Award-winning children's book author Elaine Landau worked as a newspaper reporter, a children's book editor, and a youth services librarian before becoming a full-time writer. She has written more than two hundred nonfiction books for young readers. You can visit Elaine Landau at her website: www.elainelandau.com.

PHOTO ACKNOWLEDGMENTS

The images in this book are used with the permission of: © Owaki-Kulla/CORBIS, pp. 4–5; © Publiphoto/Photo Researchers, Inc., p. 6; © Volker Steger/Nordstar/Photo Researchers, Inc., p. 8; Library of Congress, pp. 11 (LC-DIG-ppmsc-05874), 23 (LC-USZ62-70302); © age fotostock/SuperStock pp. 12, 14, 39, 46–47; © Charles E. Rotkin/CORBIS, p. 16; The Illustrated London News, p. 18; © SIBL/New York Public Library/Photo Researchers, Inc., p. 20; © Underwood Photo Archives/SuperStock, p. 25; © The Granger Collection, New York, p. 27; © Bettmann/CORBIS, pp. 28, 34; © Jerry Amster/SuperStock, p. 32; National Park Service, Museum Management Program and Edison National Historic Site, p. 36; © National Archives, p. 40; © SuperStock, Inc./SuperStock, p. 41; © Robert Llewellyn/SuperStock, p. 43; © Reuters/CORBIS, p. 44. Front cover: top, © Michael T. Sedam/CORBIS; bottom, © Royalty-Free/Corbis. Montgomery Ward & Co., back cover, p. 1, all borders.